FACT FRENZY

ANIMAL FACT FRENZY!

by Cari Meister

CAPSTONE PRESS
a capstone imprint

Published by Capstone Press, an imprint of Capstone
1710 Roe Crest Drive, North Mankato, Minnesota 56003
capstonepub.com

Animal Fact Frenzy! was originally published as *Totally Wacky Facts About Sea Animals* and *Totally Wacky Facts About Land Animals*, copyright 2016 by Capstone Press.

Library of Congress Cataloging-in-Publication Data
is available on the Library of Congress website.

ISBN: 9798875254642 (hardcover)
ISBN: 9798875254598 (paperback)
ISBN: 9798875254604 (ebook PDF)

Summary: There's an ANIMAL FACT FRENZY headed your way! Did you know that hagfish tie themselves in knots to keep from being eaten? Or that there's an adorable animal that poops 40 times a day? Dozens of bite-size facts are paired with incredible photos, welcoming in even the most reluctant readers. Whether kids are in the mood to browse or to devour a book from cover to cover, they're sure to learn some fascinating animal facts as they fly through these pages.

Editorial Credits
Designers: Jaime Willems and Tracy Davies; Media Researcher: Svetlana Zhurkin; Production Specialist: Whitney Schaefer

Image Credits
Alamy: David Fleetham, 49 (top), John Cancalosi, 41; Getty Images: 3dsam79, 8, Andyworks, 37 (top), ArtyuStudio, 5 (shark), bbevren, 25 (top), Buena Vista Images, 15 (middle), Cindy Kassab, 11, David Butler, 37 (bottom), David Keep, 57, Gerald Corsi, 10 (bottom), Ian_Redding, 60 (top), ifish, 15 (top), James R.D. Scott, 26 (bottom), JasonOndreicka, 39 (top), Martin Harvey, 60 (middle), Paul Souders, 20, torstenvelden, 22, towlake, 63, USO, 58, Utopia_88, 55, Vac1, 19, ValerieVS, 42, Yiming Chen, 30 (isopod); Shutterstock: Acon Cheng, 46 (middle), Alex Popov, 30 (tray), Animanish, 23 (top), Anna L. e Marina Durante, 26 (top right), barbaliss, 5 (top back), bilalwebdesigner, 1 (bottom), 23 (bottom), Brent Barnes, 21 (bottom), chimpokamon, cover (bottom left), Chris Fourie, 61, Christos Georghiou, 3, 35 (bottom), CK Ma, 49 (bottom), CkyBe (speech bubble), 5 and throughout, Danny Ye, 44 (middle), Diana Taliun, 28 (bottom), Diego Grandi, 18 (middle), DJ Mattaar, 14, Eric Isselee, cover (bottom right), 4 (left), 5 (bottom), 51 (bottom), 64, fivespots, 31 (bottom), Gallwis, 31 (top), Gennaro DiBs, 50 (bottom), gn8 (rays and lines), cover and throughout, Guppic the duck, cover (hats, glasses), Iyoob, 59 (top), Ken Griffiths, 47, Kim_Briers, 43 (bottom), Kurit afshen, 9, Lukas Kovarik, cover (top left), maheki, 53 (bottom), Margaret M Stewart, 54 (bottom), Martin Mecnarowski, 35 (top), Matt Jeppson, 38, Meda01, 17 (bottom), mentalmind, 59 (mosquitoes), Milan Zygmunt, 7, MLeCharpentier, 28 (middle), Nataliia Volyk (animal icons), cover, back cover, Nattapon Siansawat, 24, NatureDiver, 29, Net Vector, 40 (top), pan demin, cover (top right), Parinussa Revy, 50 (top), Paulpixs, 17 (middle), Philippe Clement, 18 (bottom), Piotr Poznan, 32 (hummingbird), pixelpics, 16, pr2is, 25 (bottom), Rabia Yousaf, 21 (top), Rich Carey, back cover, 4 (right), Richard Whitcombe, 62, Rosa Jay, 4 (middle), Rudmer Zwerver (bat), 1, 59, SanderMeertinsPhotography, 52, Sascha Janson, 45, schankz, 13, Scisetti Alfio, 54 (top), Sensvector, 26 (top left), Sergey Uryadnikov, 12, stephan kerkhofs, 51 (top), Steve Bower, cover (middle left), Stu Porter, 34, Sudowoodo, 53 (top), Sumaira35, 6, Tamer A Soliman, 39 (bottom), Tesalonika tengker, 27, Thierry Eidenweil, 33, Tom Clausen, 36, TotemArt, 44 (bottom), 46 (top), v_kulieva (gradient background), back cover and throughout, Vidyaskannan, 10 (middle), Wojciech Boruch, 32 (coin); SuperStock: BlueGreen Pictures, 56, Minden Pictures, 40 (middle), Norbert Wu, 48

Printed in the United States 6739

TABLE OF CONTENTS

AN ANIMAL-TASTIC FACT COLLECTION!

Been to the zoo lately? Looked under a bush or up a tree? Seen any ants invading your kitchen? Near and far, we're surrounded by beasties. From fascinating to frightfully foul, the world is full of fishy, feathered, flying, and furry friends . . . and foes. Find out who's fastest, who's fiercest, and who's most likely to electrocute you in this untamed collection of facts about the wild creatures among us.

GET READY FOR A FRENZY OF ANIMAL FACTS YOU'LL NEVER FORGET!

CREATURE FEATURES, TALENTS, AND TRAITS

The cheetah clocks in as the fastest mammal, running 70 miles (113 kilometers) per hour.

The peregrine falcon can reach speeds of up to 200 miles (322 km) per hour!

The three-toed sloth is the slowest animal. It moves so little that algae grows on its fur.

The barreleye fish has a see-through head.

One kind of icefish has see-through blood.

Octopuses, lobsters, and squid have blue blood.

A kind of skink lizard has green blood.

Male "dancing frogs" wave their legs in the air to attract mates.

Flying fish use their pectoral fins to glide through the air.

A penguin can't fly, but it can jump 6 feet (1.8 meters) in the air from the water!

Great white sharks can launch themselves 8 to 10 feet (2.4 to 3 m) into the air.

Elephants are one of the only land mammals that can't jump.

WOW!

KANGAROOS CAN TRAVEL 25 FEET (7.6 M) IN ONE LEAP. BUT THEY CAN'T RUN.

Parrotfish eat coral and poop sand. One parrotfish poops about 220 pounds (100 kilograms) or more of sand per year!

Pandas poop about 40 times per day.

Sea flatworms poop out of their mouths.

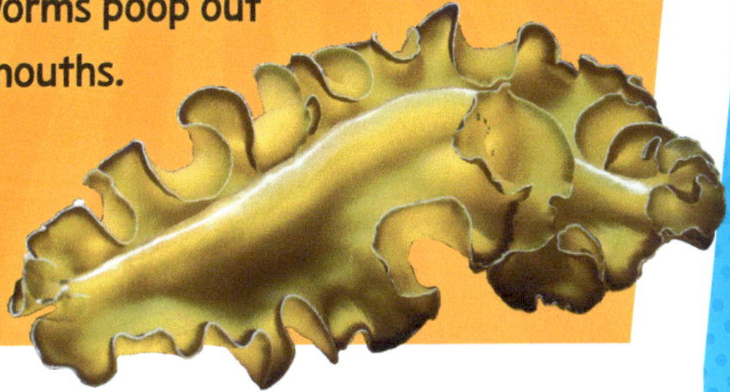

WOW!

HIPPOS FLING POOP AT EACH OTHER WHEN GETTING OUT OF THE WATER.

Vultures pee on their legs to keep cool. It's natural air-conditioning!

Flies lay their eggs in rotting flesh.

Houseflies hum in the key of F!

A viperfish has fangs so long that they don't fit in its mouth.

An alligator can regrow one tooth 50 times.

WOW!

A NARWHAL'S TUSK IS REALLY A TOOTH THAT GROWS THROUGH ITS LIP.

A walrus' teeth can break through 8 inches (20 centimeters) of ice.

A walrus' mating call sounds like a bell ringing.

The oyster toadfish looks like a toad and sounds like a foghorn.

WILD, SIZE-WISE

The largest fish in the sea, the whale shark, is longer than a school bus.

A manatee's intestines can be as long as three-and-a-half school buses!

A bull shark can weigh almost as much as a grand piano.

The ocean sunfish can weigh up to 5,000 pounds (2,268 kg).

The height of a male orca's dorsal fin is 6 feet (1.8 m) tall.

The Japanese spider crab can measure 12 feet (3.7 m) from claw to claw!

A tuna's eye is nearly the size of a baseball.

A colossal squid's eye is the size of a dinner plate.

A sperm whale's brain is five times larger than a human's.

WOW!

A TARSIER'S EYE IS BIGGER THAN ITS BRAIN.

A blue whale is about 25 feet (7.6 m) long when it's born—the length of two cars!

A newborn seahorse is the size of one jelly bean.

The largest sea star is 3.3 feet (1 m) across. The smallest is about 0.5 inches (1.3 cm) across.

The giant isopod can be 16 inches (41 cm)—about the size of a lunch tray.

Giant tubeworms grow to be 8 feet (2.4 m) long.

Reticulated pythons can grow as long as 32 feet (9.8 m)!

Some hummingbirds weigh
less than a penny.

A bumblebee bat is the world's smallest mammal. It's as heavy as two paperclips.

An octopus can squeeze through any opening bigger than its beak.

Tusks are really very large teeth. An elephant's tusks can grow to be 10 feet (3 m) long.

A newborn elephant can weigh 200 pounds (91 kg).

40,000: the number of muscles in an elephant's trunk

A bald eagle's nest can be more than 9 feet (2.7 m) across and 20 feet (6 m) tall.

One underground prairie dog town covered 25,000 square miles (64,750 square km)!

WICKED WEAPONRY AND DEFENSES

Hognose snakes let out stinky "death" smells to avoid capture.

An opossum will play dead for hours, even sticking out its tongue for added effect.

WOW!

Some sea cucumbers look like poop.

Some kinds of carpenter ants purposely explode with toxic goo to stop predators.

A vulture barfs to keep enemies at bay.

WOW!

THE HORNED LIZARD CAN SHOOT BLOOD OUT OF ITS EYES.

The Moroccan flic-flac spider back-handsprings away from its enemies.

The snapping shrimp uses one of its claws as a water pistol.

A mantis shrimp can punch with the force of a speeding bullet.

A sun jellyfish has poisonous tentacles that are more than 120 feet (37 m) long.

Electric eels create up to 600 volts of electricity—enough to shock a person to death.

It would take just a few minutes for the toxins from a blue-ringed octopus to kill a person.

The venom in a box jellyfish can stop a person's heart within minutes!

The poison in one pufferfish
can kill 30 people.

WOW!

ONE BITE FROM AUSTRALIA'S INLAND TAIPAN SNAKE CONTAINS ENOUGH VENOM TO KILL 100 PEOPLE.

Hagfish tie themselves in knots to keep from being eaten.

If an octopus loses an arm, a new one grows.

If a flatworm is cut in half, each half will become a whole new worm.

The peanut worm can pull its head and tentacles inside its body.

Cuttlefish can change color to match their surroundings.

A mimic octopus can change its shape and color to look like a lionfish.

WHAT'S FOR DINNER?

Egyptian vultures use rocks to break open ostrich eggs.

The American burying beetle buries dead birds and rodents for its babies to eat.

Flies eat poop.

A capybara eats its own poop.

A chipmunk's cheek pouches can hold about 32 beechnuts.

Many snakes are able to stretch their lower jaws so they can swallow large animals whole.

Owls swallow their food whole and then cough up pellets of bones and fur.

Deep-sea dragonfish wave around a lighted barbel to attract food.

Orcas slap the water's surface to make waves that knock animals off the ice. Then the orcas feast!

A seal's whiskers can sense a fish swimming 600 feet (183 m) away.

A great white shark can smell blood a quarter mile (0.4 km) away. It can also eat a seal in 10 bites!

A sperm whale eats more than 5,000 squid in one week.

A blue whale eats 40 million krill in one day.

In a study, bats ate up to 1,000 mosquitoes in one hour.

Sea woodlice attach themselves to a fish's tongue and then suck out its blood.

Monkeys pick (and eat) bugs out of each other's hair.

A sperm whale eats more than 5,000 squid in one week.

A blue whale eats 40 million krill in one day.

In a study, bats ate up to 1,000 mosquitoes in one hour.

Sea woodlice attach themselves to a fish's tongue and then suck out its blood.

Monkeys pick (and eat) bugs out of each other's hair.

A jackal cub eats its mom's barf.

Octopuses taste food with suction cups that line each of their arms.

When a colossal squid swallows prey, the food enters its brain before its stomach.

When a sea star eats, its stomach pops out of its body!

BOOKS IN THIS SERIES